AF584558

NP
NP

Vietnam MiG Killers

Deadly duel over Vietnam

Robert F. Dorr

First published in 1988 by Motorbooks International Publishers & Wholesalers Inc, P O Box 2, 729 Prospect Avenue, Osceola, WI 54020 USA

Printed and bound in Hong Kong

Library of Congress Cataloging-in-Publication Data
Dorr, Robert F.
Vietnam MiG killers

1. Vietnamese Conflict, 1961-1975—Aerial operations, American. 2. Airplanes, Military—United States.
I. Title.
DS558.8.D67 1988 959.704'348 87-35670
ISBN 0-87938-286-4

On the front cover: *The Air Force's first MiG killers. Standing in front of a gull-gray F-4C Phantom of the 45th TFS at Ubon, the airmen who bagged two MiG-17s on July 10, 1965, are in a festive mood. The four men in two Phantoms who scored these victories all left the Air Force afterward and identifying them two decades later is not easy, but included in this group are Captains Kenneth E. Holcombe, Arthur C. Clark, Thomas S. Roberts and Ronald C. Anderson.* US Air Force

On the frontispiece: *During the Eleven Day War of December 18-29, 1972, the Strategic Air Command's stark black B-52D Stratofortresses pounded Hanoi and shot down two MiG-21s. Aircraft 55-0057, on display at Maxwell AFB, Alabama, on April 27, 1987, is identical to airplanes 55-083 and 56-676 of the 307th Strategic Wing, which shot down the MiGs.* Robert F. Dorr

On the title page: *F-8E Crusader of the "Checkmates" of fighter squadron VF-211 launches for North Vietnam from the deck of USS* Bon Homme Richard *(CVA-31) in 1968. Though its four 20-mm Mark 12 cannons were cantankerous and difficult to use, pilots felt that the guns gave them a better chance against the MiG-17 and MiG-21.* Ron Lord

On the contents page: *F-4C Phantom 64-0660 was a triple MiG killer—and proud of its splitter-plate kill markings.* Bill Spidle

On the back cover: *BUCKET 01 was the radio callsign for F-4D Phantom 66-0240 on December 21, 1972, when the crew destroyed a MiG-21 without firing a shot. Captain Gary L. Sholders and 1st Lt. Eldon D. Brinkley of the "Triple Nickel" 555th Tactical Fighter Squadron were up north during the Christmas bombing when they maneuvered the MiG into crashing to earth. As depicted subsequently on September 18, 1978, their Phantom served with the 44th TFS at Kadena Field, Okinawa.* Masumi Wada

COL. R. C. BEYER
EJECTION SEAT AND CANOPY
CAUTION
MIG-17
MIG-17
MIG-17
ACFT
666

Contents

High-spirited paintbrush artists found various ways to indicate MiG kills on the aircraft which scored them. Hash marks, recognition silhouettes of a MiG-17 and even the North Vietnamese flag all appeared at one time or another. On F-105D Thunderchief 61-0069, callsign HAMBONE 03 on June 3, 1967, when Captain Larry D. Wiggins shot down a MiG-17 using both cannon and a Sidewinder missile, the MiG kill stayed on long after the other artwork offended a senior officer and had to be removed. When Wiggins' Thud was restored at Norton AFB, California, on October 25, 1983, the paint scheme was historically accurate—but, again, Cherry Girl *had to be removed after a few days.* Donald S. McGarry

Menace of the MiG

A MiG in a museum. A tiny red star glinting on the splitter plate of a Phantom. A memory. This is all that remains now of an air war in which the best and brightest fought in vast yawning skies above the most heavily-defended real estate on earth, pitting themselves and their machines against an entrenched and determined enemy.

Kill MiGs. Every last fighter jock who ever went into the Hanoi-Haiphong region of North Vietnam wanted, more than anything, to kill MiGs.

Air-to-air combat has always been the ultimate test for the fighter pilot and, despite its savagery, has always possessed a certain nobility of purpose. It is personal. It is so intensely personal that American fighter wing commander Robin Olds often contemplated his counterpart, North Vietnamese fighter regiment leader Colonel Nguyen Van Huu, and wondered what it would be like to meet and talk.

The checkered scarves and chivalry of the biplane air battles of 1917-18 might have become history in the meanwhile—although Captain Steve Ritchie wore such a scarf, and men still observed the nicety of not shooting each other in their parachutes—but the act of pitting oneself and one's Thud, Phantom or Crusader against an enemy in a MiG-17 or MiG-21 remained the ultimate test. One pilot with a literary bent compared the American fighter pilot up near Hanoi with Hemingway's matador confronting death in the afternoon.

In the larger scheme of things, air-to-air combat over North Vietnam was far less important as a military proposition. The United States fought three major campaigns over North Vietnam; Rolling Thunder from March 2, 1965, to October 3, 1968; Linebacker from May 8, 1972, to October 18, 1972; and Linebacker II from December 18 to December 29, 1972. Further actions took place during the long intervals of "bombing halts."

At least 10,000 men flew combat missions up north and of these, fewer than 500 ever saw a MiG; only 170 shot one down. The principal purpose of the missions up north was to drop bombs and to choke off the enemy's supply line to the communist insurgency in South Vietnam. Even when MiG kills were scored, as in Operation Bolo on January 2, 1967, when Colonel Olds' Phantoms shot down seven MiG-21s in one engagement, it usually happened in the sky because the Americans were prohibited by the rules of engagement from catching MiGs on the ground.

Most fighter pilots carried bombs and attacked supply depots, petroleum facilities and bridges. Colonel Doug Carter, who flew 227 Phantom missions, summed up his experience by expressing his satisfaction over using the latest electro-optical-guided bombs. The breaking of the Thanh Hoa Bridge, the mining of Haiphong harbor and the bombing of petroleum facilities were examples of major achievements directly related to the purpose of the US war effort.

But it was always the MiG which captured the imagination of the American fighter pilot. Beginning in 1964-65 when a cadre of Soviet-trained North Vietnamese pilots set up shop with a few vintage 1950s MiG-17s, Hanoi rapidly built up a formidable, highly disciplined and very able fighter force which eventually employed seven principal airfields and 200 MiG-17s, MiG-19s and MiG-21s. Ho Chi Minh's air defense network grew to include ninety SAM sites and 1,900 anti-aircraft guns. The heartland of North Vietnam, which the Americans called Route Package Six, became the most fiercely defended real estate on earth. It was the MiG pilot who challenged the man in an F-105, F-4 or F-8 to fight and win.

Nor was the aging MiG-17 any pushover. Americans went to war in 1965 trained to believe that fighters were getting faster and faster, many easily exceeding Mach Two, and that engagements would take place at greater ranges, with kills being racked up by air-to-air missiles at enormous distances, sometimes beyond visual range.

Phantoms went to war armed with AIM-7 radar-guided missiles effective at up to eighteen miles, giving them a head-to-head capability which the North Vietnamese never possessed throughout the conflict but which, in the end, rarely did them much good. The Phantom's secondary armament of AIM-9 Sidewinder heat-seeking missiles, effective only from behind the heat source of the enemy's exhaust, killed more MiGs. Thuds and Crusaders at least had guns, which the Phantom lacked.

The relatively slow MiG-17, which never had a radar-guided missile and only rarely packed the heat-seeking Atoll, possessed the "right stuff" for engagements which were fought not at great distances but at close range, not at Mach Two but at subsonic speed, not with electronic "black boxes" but with the human eyeball, not with missiles but with guns. Above all, the MiG-17 fought and often won because it was lightweight, nimble and very maneuverable. The MiG-21 came from a later generation and was more likely to have missiles as well as guns, but it was the maneuverability of the MiG-17 which proved the Americans' greatest challenge.

It should be remembered that the Americans had to travel far to engage the enemy, lugging external fuel tanks and refueling in midair routinely for the first time in any war, while their wily adversary was fighting over his homeland and could be airborne in seconds, in "clean" condition. The Americans also faced missiles and Triple-As while the North Vietnamese concentrated exclusively on air-to-air engagements. While history often favors he who attacks, in this instance the defenders had every advantage.

It is a tribute to the fighting spirit of all who ventured up north that American fighter pilots shot down 195 MiGs (and two Antonov An-2 biplanes) with losses of only eighty-nine aircraft in air-to-air combat. Toward the end of the war, largely thanks to air combat maneuver training taking place at the Navy Fighter Weapons School, known as Top Gun, American pilots were performing far better than the 197:89 ratio suggests. It took courage, skill and tenacity to face up to the MiG.

Despite its age, the MiG-17 was a formidable opponent. Based upon the MiG-15 which had been successful during the Korean War and powered by a 7,500-lb. thrust Klimov VK-1 afterburning turbojet, the cannon-armed MiG-17 was the most maneuverable fighter in the skies above North Vietnam. This example was donated to the Fighter Aces Museum in Champlin, Arizona, by the King of Morocco. Douglas E. Slowiak

FJ

DISTRICT OF COLUMBIA AIR NATIONAL GUARD

Thud up north

It was big. It was mean. Everybody knew it. With a fuselage length of 64 ft. 4 in., the Republic F-105D Thunderchief—known, evermore, as the Thud—was longer than a Catalina and only a few inches shorter than a DC-3.

The Thud had been built as a nuclear bomber with a gaping twenty-foot internal weapons bay. Designed by a team headed by Alexander Kartveli, who also created the P-47 Thunderbolt and F-84 Thunderjet, the Thud departed on a combat mission at a gross weight of no less than 52,500 lb. and could climb to 35,200 feet in its first minute of flight.

Powered by a Pratt & Whitney J75-P-19W turbojet rated at 24,000 lb. static thrust with afterburner and 26,400 lb. with water injection, the Thud was never intended for air-to-air combat but became an aerial opponent of the MiG nevertheless. In the air-to-air role, the F-105D carried an M61A1 rotary cannon with 1,000 rounds and could be equipped with two AIM-9D Sidewinders.

In what amounted to a sort of mini-Pearl Harbor, the first air-to-air kills of the Southeast Asia war were not MiGs but Thuds. On April 4, 1965, as Lt. Col. Robinson Risner's 67th Tactical Fighter Squadron assaulted the Thanh Hoa Bridge, two Thuds of ZINC Flight were ambushed from behind by a pair of MiG-17s. Laden with bombs and wholly unprepared, the two Thuds were blasted out of the sky before they could defend themselves.

It did not happen again. In fact, the Republic F-105 Thunderchief went on to establish itself as the mount of some genuine American heroes.

Captain Max C. Brestel shot down two MiG-17s with 20-mm cannon fire on March 10, 1967, making

After the war, the F-105D Thunderchief served admirably with Air Force Reserve and Air National Guard units. Aircraft 58-1155, here, has its 20-mm cannon access doors open for service and provides a rare view of the internal fuel tank occupying the Thud fuselage space originally intended as an internal bomb bay. Another District of Columbia Guard aircraft, 60-504, was credited with two MiGs. Robert F. Dorr

Into the crucible. At the controls of a single-seat F-105D, Captain Donald L. Heiliger heads into North Vietnam in April 1966, loosely packed and looking for trouble from Uncle Ho's MiGs. Without bombload, Heiliger should give a good account of himself if a MiG shows. Although flying with the 333rd Tactical Fighter Squadron (TFS) at Takhli, Don is wearing the "Red Dog" helmet of the 36th TFS at Yokota AB, Japan. On his second go-around in Southeast Asia, Don was hit by North Vietnamese gunfire on May 15, 1967, ejected and was a prisoner of war for the next six years.
Donald L. Heiliger

The single-seat Thud pilot was kept very busy. The pilot had to keep frequent watch on the information being given to him by his radar scope. Don Heiliger, approaching Da Nang airfield from the northeast in September 1966, had this view of the airstrip and its peninsula inside his F-105D.
Donald L. Heiliger

OFF
STEER NEEDLE
DN
80
10
LBS
FUEL
AUX
TOTAL

his the first "double score" of the conflict; he went on to complete 100 missions up north in the Thud and came back later for a second combat tour in OV-10 Broncos.

Colonel Jack Broughton, deputy commander of the 355th TFW at Takhli, got a "probable" MiG kill, won two Air Force Cross nominations for leading Thud strike forces over Hanoi and Haiphong, and later described his experiences in the volumes *Thud Ridge* and *Going Downtown.* Court-martialed for destroying gun-camera film of two of his pilots strafing a Soviet freighter in Haiphong harbor, Broughton became a hero within the Air Force for defending the men.

Persistent, courageous attacks on SAM sites in the two-seat F-105F Wild Weasel resulted in Medal of Honor awards for Captain Merlyn H. Dethlefsen on the day Brestel was getting his MiG kills and for Major Leo K. Thorsness five weeks later on April 19, 1967. Only twelve Air Force men received the nation's highest award in the entire conflict; having two Weasels on the roster was something special. Thorsness shot down a MiG-17 to boot, but was himself downed and held prisoner for six years. Colonel Risner also became a POW, and organized and led the prisoners' resistance throughout their captivity.

During the heaviest fighting up north, Thuds were fielded by two tactical fighter wings, the 355th TFW at Takhli and the 388th TFW at Korat. So much got into print about the Takhli aviators that the men at Korat called themselves the Avis Wing: in the spirit of a car rental ad of the period, they were number two and trying harder.

Yet the 388th was a full equal when it came to courage. The wing's 1st Lt. Karl Richter got a MiG on September 21, 1966, and refused to go home when his 100 missions were up. Though he stopped counting to stay in the war, Richter had logged at least 175 missions when he was shot down. Though a chopper crew retrieved him from a karst ridgeline, Richter died on the flight back to Korat, and many believed he should have had the Medal of Honor.

The warplane flown by these men almost defies superlatives. Everything about the Thud spelled size, strength and brute force. The joke was, you could get a MiG by taxiing over the top of him, retracting the gear and squashing the hapless enemy. One airman recalled his astonishment at first encounter when he found that he could stand fully erect under its wing and look up at it. Tales abounded of the Thud returning to base with mind-boggling battle damage—an empennage shot away, a hole in the wing large enough to crawl through. And although no one ever recorded the details, one Thud got home with an unexploded air-to-air missile imbedded deeply in its rear fuselage—not an enemy Atoll, but an American AIM-9 Sidewinder.

Close calls were the stuff of the Thud pilot's life, and many a senior colonel or newly-starred BG is able to walk the halls of the Pentagon today because his thirty-ton lead sled made it home with punctured hydraulics, a shot-out electrical system or a stabilator hanging loose in broken fragments.

Captain Dave Roeder of the 388th TFW took a 7.62-mm shell fragment which shattered his canopy and inflicted a harmless but effusive cut to the back of his neck. After taxiing in at Korat, Roeder scared the daylights out of his crewchief by handing over his helmet, whereupon both men discovered a pool of blood sloshing around inside.

Max C. Brestel, right, was the Air Force's top MiG killer when he claimed two MiG-17s in a battle near Hanoi on March 10, 1967. Like most men who flew the Thud, Brestel was enthusiastic about the F-105. But he wanted to return to the combat zone badly enough to take a second tour in the "bug smasher" OV-10 Bronco. In 1971 at Nakhon Phanom, Thailand, he congratulates a fellow Bronco jock on completing a tour. **Arnie Franklin**

PICK UP F.O.D.

RU
AF
61
069

Previous page

Another view of MiG-killing Thud 61-0069 flown by Captain Larry D. Wiggins on his June 3, 1967, aerial victory. Preserved at Norton AFB, California, the aircraft kept this authentic recreation of its Vietnam paint scheme only very briefly. Donald S. McGarry

On an early Rolling Thunder mission against North Vietnam in 1965, an F-105D Thunderchief (62-4405) escorts a tanker while en route to Hanoi. This Thud was shot down by groundfire on March 5, 1967. What appears to be unusual fairing beneath the Thud's nose is, in fact, the snout of an accompanying F-4C Phantom (63-7683) which, although hidden in the background here, went on to shoot down a MiG-21 during Colonel Robin Olds' celebrated Operation Bolo on January 2, 1967.

24405

HANOI HUSTLER

WW
AF
63
320

Previous page
Hanoi Hustler, *a two-seat F-105F Wild Weasel (63-8320), wears three MiG kills to accompany its shark's teeth. The marking apparently represents the total of three MiGs downed by different F-105Fs during the conflict. Plane 820 can only claim one-half of a North Vietnamese MiG-17 in its own right. On December 19, 1967, crewed by Majors William M. Dalton and James L. Graham, this elongated Thud shared the dispatch of a MiG-17 with an F-4D Phantom flown by Major Joseph D. Moore and 1st Lt. George H. McKinney, Jr. With the addition of QRC-380 electronic blisters on the fuselage, the aircraft had been converted to F-105G standard when seen at George AFB, California, on April 25, 1980.* Donald S. McGarry

Some Thuds accumulated very high airframe hours before reaching the end of their service lives. F-105D Thunderchief 62-4361 fought through the heavy aerial campaigns of 1967-68 and survived to join the Air Force Reserve at Hill AFB, Utah. Seen with black tailcodes adopted after the end of the conflict, 361 goes into a gentle bank on a mission from Hill on September 28, 1983.

HI
AF
62 361
AFRES

NP
147021
USS BON HOMME RICHARD
NAVY
VF-24
448
04
NP
149220
USS BON HOMME RICHARD
NAVY
VF-211
04

Carrier war

Yankee Station was a region (not a fixed spot) in the Gulf of Tonkin, but it was also a state of mind. Operations from an aircraft carrier deck mean inherent danger even in peacetime, inevitable danger in an environment where high-speed aircraft and the equipment used to launch and recover them must be manned in all weather, day and night, and a "dead catapult" shot or a "bolter" (going around the pattern after a missed approach) place enormous demands on all involved.

Merely working on a carrier involved weeks and months of seaborne operations in which routine dangers were faced routinely, while incredibly demanding maintenance tasks had to be performed at all hours under all conditions. Fighters from the USS *Midway* (CVA-41) scored the first and last MiG kills of the war, and in between thousands of men labored and sacrificed to send a few dozen flying into the missiles, MiGs and Triple-As of North Vietnam.

"When you're out of F-8s, you're out of fighters." So went the litany of those who flew the much-loved and possibly over-rated Vought F-8 Crusader, usually from smaller *Essex*-class carriers which could not accommodate Phantoms. The Crusader seemed to embody everything a fighter pilot wanted: single-seat, single-engine, highly maneuverable and, above all, armed with guns. The truth was, the Crusader's four 20-mm cannons were not as effective as the Thud's one, and the Crusader's single pair of eyeballs were not as effective in spotting Comrade Tomb coming as the Phantom's two. But Crusader pilots were a

Into harm's way. USS Bon Homme Richard *(CVA-31) passes the Arizona memorial at Pearl Harbor en route to war. "Bonnie Dick" was to muster two F-8 Crusader squadrons against the North Vietnamese MiG threat, the "Renegades" of VF-24, upper right, and the "Checkmates" of VF-211, center. Both did well. In all, Crusaders shot down twenty MiGs during the conflict. These squadrons accounted for thirteen of the twenty.*
Ron Lord

dedicated, spirited lot, unquestionably possessed of a fine air combat machine and they used it to advantage.

Designed by a team under Vought's Russell Clark and first flown at Edwards AFB, California, on March 25, 1955, by John Konrad, the Crusader was powered by an 11,000-lb. thrust Pratt & Whitney J57-P-12 turbojet with afterburner. It featured a high, sweptback wing which could be cranked up or down to change the angle of attack; up for low-speed carrier landings, down for supersonic flight. On August 21, 1956, a production Crusader flown by Commander R. W. (Duke) Windsor set a world speed record of 1,015 mph.

Reconnaissance versions, the RF-8A and RF-8G, fought in Southeast Asia from beginning to end. Numerous rebuilds of the basic design fought in Vietnam, including the F-8E model having a hardened wing for air-to-ground ordnance. Marines flew the Crusader from land bases during the conflict, although the Navy's carrier-based F-8s were the only Crusaders to get MiGs.

One triumph for the Crusader was the final MiG shot down in the 1965-68 Rolling Thunder campaign against North Vietnam, scored by the "Sundowners" of squadron VF-111 which had a detachment aboard USS *Intrepid* (CVS-11). The contest began when *Intrepid* launched a pair of "Sundowner" F-8C Crusaders piloted by Lt. j.g. Alexander Rucker and Lt. Anthony J. (Tony) Nargi. Nargi, piloting F-8C number 146981, callsign OLD NICK, led the pair over a gray, gunmetal sea and followed radio instructions to intercept two bogies.

Nargi pointed the two-plane section up through scattered cumulus, leveled off at 19,000 feet and began a ninety-degree turn toward the North Vietnamese shoreline. Halfway through the turn, he made visual contact. He and Rucker broke out of the turn, applied afterburner and closed with a lone MiG-21. The Crusader's capability for high-speed maneuver was put to the test as Nargi went into a turning contest while also entering a high-speed loop. An aural tone in his earphones told him that his heat-seeking Sidewinder had acquired the MiG. He fired and watched the missile gather speed and bore up the enemy's tailpipe. Nargi saw the MiG's canopy pop off and an instant later the pilot ejected, leaving behind a flaming wreckage which rolled over and fell from sight.

While the men who fed them, armed them and shot them off carrier decks watched and waited to learn the results of each mission, carrier aviators pressed the war. On two separate occasions, MiG-17s fell to the guns of Douglas A-1 Skyraiders, the huge, prop-driven attack planes which wheezed, belched, leaked oil furiously and weren't supposed to be able to fight jets. Even their feat was bested by the A-4C Skyhawk pilot who downed a MiG with air-to-ground Zuni rockets!

It remained for the F-4 Phantom to achieve most of the Navy's successes in combating the North Vietnamese air arm. With two engines, two men, no gun at all and a curious bent-wing appearance that made it look as if someone had dropped the blueprints, the Phantoms had been designed as a fleet defense interceptor. When Robert C. Little took the prototype for its maiden flight at St. Louis on May 27, 1958, no one dreamed that the Phantom would become a multirole machine and would prove effective against smaller, lighter jet fighters with guns.

The Navy and Marine Corps went into the war with the F-4B model powered by 12,000-lb. thrust General Electric J79-GE-8A/B engines with afterburners. As the war progressed, the F-4J version introduced 15,000-lb. thrust J79-GE-19s. But throughout the war, *any* J79 emitted a long gushing trail of black smoke, making the airplane which produced it highly visible to North Vietnamese observers, pilots and gunners—a flaw in the Phantom's design which was not corrected until after the conflict.

There were not many such flaws. The Phantom soon gained supremacy as the principal fighter aircraft of the war. The Air Force and Marine Corps used it to great advantage and it soon supplemented, then replaced, the Crusader on Navy carrier decks. At one point in 1972, just as the fighting over North Vietnam was heaviest, every single carrier deck in the Navy was equipped with Phantoms. USS *Midway*'s feat in scoring the first and last MiG kills of the war was only one of many accomplishments of the best-known and most-used fighter of all.

Sea and sky were the province of the naval aviator. The "Checkmates" of squadron VF-211, who flew this F-8E Crusader from the deck of USS Bon Homme Richard *prayed for safe haven from the dangers of both while carrying an aggressive fight into the midst of the MiG. Many accounts held that the Crusader was a formidable opponent for the MiG because, unlike the Phantom, it carried internal guns. In fact, the Crusader's four Mark 12 20-mm cannons were cantankerous and trouble-prone, and figured in only two of the Crusader's twenty MiG kills, the remainder being accomplished with the reliable AIM-9 Sidewinder missile. Even at the height of fighting, tests showed that naval aviators experienced more apprehension when coming in to land on a pitching, heaving carrier deck than when actually engaged in air-to-air combat.* Ron Lord

02
AG
8578
USS INDEPENDENCE
NAVY
148578
VA76

The Douglas A-4 Skyhawk, that lightweight attack craft so effective in air-to-ground strikes, hadn't been meant to mix it up with MiGs, but Lt. Cmdr. Theodore R. Swartz of the "Spirits" of attack squadron VA-76 paid no heed to this. Loitering over North Vietnam's Kep airfield with a load of Zuni rockets at the controls of A-4C Skyhawk 148609, Swartz found himself in a violent disagreement with a MiG-17 driver. The Zuni was an unguided, air-to-ground projectile of no value in a dogfight—but Swartz paid no heed to this either. He sent a barrage of Zunis pouring into the MiG and blew it out of the sky. Swartz' success may have had something to do with the fact that he was a Crusader jock who made the transition into Skyhawks. The "Spirits" were so elated, they painted a one-foot silhouette of the unlamented MiG-17 in brillant red paint astride the air intakes of all *of their Skyhawks, including 148578 seen on February 15, 1969, after its return to a stateside base.* Roy Lock

NP
42035

Skyhawks and Skyraiders flew punishing strike missions against North Vietnamese targets, and the A-1 Skyraider also excelled in the Rescap (rescue, combat air patrol) job, covering downed airmen and bringing in rescue forces. Nobody had ever thought that either of the Douglas aircraft would shoot down MiGs, but they did. With Skyhawks in the background, A-1H Skyraider (142035) of the "Barn Owls" of squadron VA-215 is positioned aboard USS Bon Homme Richard *(CVA-31) for a combat mission near Hanoi in 1967.* Ron Lord

Next page

The "Chargers" of VF-161 probably had the brightest paint scheme of any MiG-killing squadron to operate from the floating airfields on Yankee Station. F-4B Phantom 150407 was typical of the squadron's colorful aircraft, and was another survivor which got through both the 1965-68 and the 1972 campaigns against North Vietnam without a scratch. Plane 407 had undergone further modification to become an F-4N by the time it was seen aboard USS Midway *(CVA-41) in the Western Pacific in 1976.* Stephen W. Daniels

NF
07
F-4N
150407
VF-161
NAV

USS MIDWAY
107

Before the battle, F-4B Phantom 153009 of the "Screaming Eagles" of VF-51 was bright with color and ready for war. VF-51 had the distinction of being the only Navy fighter squadron to achieve aerial kills in World War II, the Korean War and the Vietnam War. M. J. Kasiuba

NL
3009
00
153009
BA

After the battle, F-4B Phantom 149457 has had it, looking decidedly worn out at NAS North Island, California, on November 13, 1976. Operating from USS Coral Sea *(CVA-43), 149457 was up near Hanoi on June 11, 1972, when a MiG-17 engaged Lt. Winston W. (Mad Dog) Copeland and Lt. Donald R. Bouchoux. The Phantom pilot and backseat radar intercept officer (RIO) struggled through a mid-morning engagement and used a Sidewinder to send the MiG pilot to his reunion with the then-recently deceased Ho Chi Minh.* Lars-Erik Lundin

VF-51
9457
NL

Marine pilots brought their first F-4B Phantoms into South Vietnam in April 1965 and remained in the area until August 1974. Though only one MiG was shot down by a Marine aircraft (and several others by Marine pilots serving exchange tours with the Air Force), the Corps was essential to the war. F-4B Phantom 152992 of the "Flying Eagles" of VMFA-115 operated from Da Nang and later from the Rose Garden as Marines called their parched, dusty airfield at Nam Phong, Thailand. The Phantom is seen here on a visit to NAF Atsugi, Japan, on August 24, 1974, just at the point when the last units of Marine Air withdrew from Southeast Asia. Masumi Wada

A sharkmouth appears on the nose. Just below the squadron designation VF-111, Stingray *wears two silhouettes of MiG-17s in red paint to signify the aerial victories of the unit. The number of deck crewmembers needed to send a modern jet fighter aloft, their different functions identified with color-coded work gear, is illustrated here. F-8E Crusader 146931 is about to take a steam-catapult trip on its way to Hanoi.* Robert L. Russell

STINGRAY
15
AH
146931
NAVY
VF-111
115

37425
U.S. AIR FORCE

Phantom

The first Air Force missions into North Vietnam beginning in March 1965 were flown by Thuds with fighter escort (known as MiGCAP or MiG Combat Air Patrol) provided by F-100D Super Sabres. It soon became clear that the Hun, as the F-100 was called, did not have the range, maneuverability or staying power for an air-to-air campaign against Hanoi's small but growing fighter force. The Lockheed F-104 Starfighter, a few of which had been deployed to Da Nang, proved to be even less suitable.

On April 4, 1965, the day MiG-17s shot down two Thuds and seemed to escape unscathed, one Hun pilot fired a Sidewinder at a MiG while another chased a North Vietnamese pilot almost into the ground only to lose sight of the foe and any chance of confirming a kill. At the same time, McDonnell F-4C Phantoms were already being brought into the base at Ubon, Thailand. It was clear that the Phantom was going to become the principal adversary of the MiG.

The high-spirited thirst for air-to-air combat was a hankering among the men who maintained and flew the aircraft but some practical considerations made it doubtful whether men and machines were ready. Few Phantom crews or airframes had ever actually fired a Sparrow or Sidewinder missile, and while every item of equipment was supposed to work as the brochure advertised, in real life each plane and crew was a little different from every other.

Early F-4Cs sprang wing tank leaks that required resealing after each flight and eighty-five of them developed cracked ribs on outer wing panels. Phantoms were at times grounded due to dripping potting compound. Tactics had yet to be developed to enable aircrews to fly and fight in an environment where SAMs endangered them at medium and high altitudes, guns threatened them down low, and MiG pilots continually wanted to cheat with hit-and-run tactics that fell short of a fair fight.

The first test between the Phantom and MiG came on July 10, 1965, when the 45th TFS at Ubon deliberately went up to Hanoi low and slow to lure the MiGs into another attempt at an easy pick-off. They did. Two Air Force crews consisting of Captains Kenneth E. Holcombe, Arthur C. Clark, Thomas S. Roberts and Ronald C. Anderson latched onto MiGs trying to play them for suckers, drew them into an

Previous page
When Phantoms first arrived in Southeast Asia, they were painted as the Air Force received them—white undersides, gull gray fuselage. It was the Navy's color scheme and the Air Force had adopted it to keep everything simple. The colorful Tactical Air Command badge seen on the tail of F-4C Phantom 63-7485 was also worn at the outset of the conflict. Gray paint and badge soon gave way to camouflage. This Phantom shows how they looked when the fighting started. The F-4C is carrying an underwing canister containing nineteen 2.75-inch air-to-ground rocket projectiles.

Is this the MiG killer nobody knows about? On April 4, 1965, the day of the first air-to-air losses when the North Vietnamese bushwacked two Thuds, Captain Don Kilgus was flying MiGCAP at the controls of F-100D 55-2894 of the 416th TFS, the "Silver Knights," operating from Da Nang. Kilgus latched behind a MiG-17, chased him from 20,000 feet down to about 7,000 and fired 20-mm cannon bursts which caused debris to fly loose from the MiG. Unable to delay pulling out any longer, Kilgus lost visual contact with the MiG just when he seemed to come flying apart. For years afterward, Don painted a red star on the F-100D and F-105F airplanes he flew, but the Air Force credited him only with a "probable" kill. On the public record, the Super Sabre, which was withdrawn from MiGCAP duties almost immediately, remains without a single aerial victory to its credit. Donald W. Kilgus

U.S. AIR FORCE

U.S. AIR FORCE

60886

Previous page
Wearing spurs on their heels, F-104 Starfighter pilots arrived in Vietnam itching to mix it up with MiGs, but they never did. Dubbed a "missile with a man in it" in the fifties, the F-104 lacked range for combat operations over North Vietnam and was not even equipped with a radar warning receiver (RWR) to alert the pilot when enemy missile sites were stalking him. After a few brief forays into North Vietnam and one or two inconclusive tangles with MiGs, the F-104 was withdrawn. Monsoon clouds form behind Fannie, *an F-104C Starfighter (56-886) of the 479th TFW at Da Nang in April 1965. Summarized a pilot of another fighter: "They never had a mission and they never made a mark."* David W. Menard

Phantom. It was the standard against which every other fighter in the world would be compared throughout the second half of the Twentieth Century. If a handful of immortals had to be named—Spitfire, Mustang, Sabre—there was no way to finish the task without including Phantom. McDonnell and Mitsubishi rolled 5,201 of them off production lines over more than twenty years and they served with twelve air forces. F-4C Phantom 64-831 got through the Vietnam conflict and eventually served with the Hawaii Air National Guard, where it wore the air defense gray paint scheme when seen on July 29, 1984. Robert F. Dorr

engagement and banged down two MiG-17s with Sidewinders.

To its credit, the Air Force embarked on a program called Charging Sparrow which required every Phantom crew in Southeast Asia to get over to Clark Field, Philippines, to acquire real experience firing the air-to-air radar-guided Sparrow. To some extent, the benefit was negated by rules of engagement which, in heavily crowded skies, prohibited using the Sparrow beyond visual range (BVR). Being required to visually identify a MiG before engaging it virtually canceled out the advantages of a radar-guided missile, something the North Vietnamese never had, and a considerable part of the fighting ultimately took place at closer distances with Sidewinders and guns.

As North Vietnam's arsenal grew, the delta-winged MiG-21 entered the fray. It was newer and faster than the MiG-17 but not as maneuverable and it never became the favorite of Hanoi's pilots. On April 29, 1966, a Phantom crew consisting of Major Paul T. Gilmore and 1st Lt. William T. Smith became the first to shoot down a MiG-21, using a Sidewinder.

As the Rolling Thunder campaign continued over North Vietnam, Air Force planners were dissatisfied that they were only racking up slightly more than one MiG kill for each aerial loss. In Korea, F-86 Sabres had killed seven MiGs for each casualty. Colonel Robin Olds came to the 8th TFW (the "Wolfpack") at Ubon determined to fare better against his North Vietnamese counterpart, Colonel Tomb. Prohibited by those same rules of engagement from attacking MiGs on the ground in their airfield revetments, Olds set up Operation Bolo to lure the North Vietnamese into the sky.

Operation Bolo was launched on January 2, 1967. The tactic was identical to that employed during the first kills of the war. Colonel Olds' F-4C Phantoms went north flying at slow speed to masquerade as bomb-laden Thuds, baiting the MiGs. When a force of MiG-21s broke into sunlight over the low cloud hugging North Vietnam, Olds' Phantom crews discarded drop tanks, went into "clean" condition and launched into abrupt maneuvers which led to prolonged, violent fighting. Olds himself had his Phantom in an energy-draining climb and went "over the top" to attack a MiG while boring down on him at an inverted angle.

When the Phantoms recovered at Ubon, they had shot down no fewer than seven MiG-21s with no losses, the best such tally of the war.

When he wasn't fuming about the AIM-4 Falcon missile which was briefly employed in the conflict and proved to be utterly useless, Olds was vehement about a gun: "I want a gun on that airplane." Finally, belly-tank SUU-16 gun pods were made available for the F-4D Phantom. In May 1967, Lt. Col. Robert F. Titus and his backseater 1st Lt. Milan Zimer accomplished the almost incredible feat in three days' time of shooting down three MiGs using all three systems—Sparrow, Sidewinder and 20-mm cannon.

The F-4E model of the Phantom with an internal 20-mm cannon—a feature the Navy never adopted—began to arrive in the war zone just as President Johnson ended the Rolling Thunder campaign with his October 31, 1968, bombing halt. When American pilots went north again in 1972, better training and separation of combat roles (with one wing assigned MiGCAP, another assigned to carry bombs) proved to be as effective as the 20-mm gun in producing a more favorable ratio of air-to-air combat successes.

The bombing halt cut off the contest between the American fighter crew and the North Vietnamese MiG pilot, but it did not prevent men from wanting to achieve a special distinction always possible in previous wars. Everybody wanted to get five aerial victories to become an ace.

It did not happen by the time North Vietnam was closed off to American warplanes on October 31, 1968. Olds got four MiGs, Titus three, Brestel two; but it looked as if the Vietnam conflict was going to grind on without anyone becoming an ace. Olds missed one opportunity when a flight of Thuds went past on full afterburner while he was setting up a shot at a MiG with a Sidewinder. He lifted his thumb from the trigger out of fear that the heat-seeking missile might go after the Thud tailpipes rather than the MiG. The chance was gone and it did not seem likely to recur.

U.S. AIR FORCE
FW-951
629

When the bombing of North Vietnam began in earnest in February 1965, the only fighter immediately available to fly escort (MiGCAP) and protect strike forces was the North American F-100D Super Sabre. The Hun, as pilots called it, was a much-loved and thoroughly capable fighter-bomber, but it was not the ideal machine for air-to-air combat and spent most of the conflict being used as a "mud mover," striking ground targets inside South Vietnam. At Da Nang in early 1965, there was a not-very-friendly competition between F-100D and F-104C pilots to see who might bag a MiG first. F-100D 56-2951 of the 615th TFS taxies at Da Nang in May 1965. David W. Menard

The red badge of courage that every Phantom pilot wanted to wear was the five-pointed star that marked a MiG kill and was painted on the air intake splitter plate of the aircraft. Red stars marking two of Colonel Robin Olds' four MiG victories appear on his F-4C Phantom 64-829 which survived the war, soldiered on for nearly two decades and ended up at the Air Force Museum in Dayton, Ohio. Where possible, purists always tried to make certain that the stars appeared on the aircraft which had actually scored the kill, but in many instances they were painted on other aircraft flown by the victorious pilot. In the two-seat Phantom, as in two-seat versions of the Thud, both front- and backseater received full credit for each MiG shot down. R. J. Mills, Jr.

Robin Olds' 64-829 went from Vietnam to Torrejon, Spain, to Homestead AFB, Florida, to Kelly Field, Texas, before ending up at the Air Force Museum. Seen making a visit to Holloman AFB, New Mexico, on August 18, 1979, during its service with the Air Reserve's 93rd TFS at Homestead, the aircraft wears Olds' two MiG kills and still has the camouflage pattern employed during the war: two shades of green-brown on top and light-colored undersides. R. J. Mills, Jr.

FM
AF
64829
AFRES
DANGER
ARRESTING HOOK

F-4C Phantom 63-7647 got through the fighting and served after the conflict with the 199th Tactical Fighter Squadron, Hawaii Air National Guard, where it is shown here at Hickam AFB, Hawaii, on July 29, 1984. In addition to postwar wraparound camouflage, it wears two red stars. Major Richard M. Pascoe and Captain Norman E. Wells of the "Triple Nickel" 555th TFS, then a part of Colonel Robin Olds' 8th TFW, scored two MiG kills but only one of them was accomplished in 647. It happened on June 5, 1967, when Pascoe and Wells, using the callsign CHICAGO 02, while on Olds' wing, spotted four MiG-17s attacking another flight up ahead. Olds went after one of the MiGs and fired all of his missiles without hitting. Pascoe then engaged one of the MiGs from a distance of five miles and fired two Sidewinders at it. Both hit the mark. The MiG-17 went into a left descending turn and struck the ground. Although the canopy left the aircraft, no parachute was observed. Robert F. Dorr

'ALAE 'OLA
CLINT CHURCHILL A.C.
STAN OSSERMAN W.S.O.
PUSH TO OPEN DOOR
CANOPY JETTISON
RESCUE

FO
AF
67
569
RESCUE

FO
AF
67
661

Previous page

The F-4D was the first Phantom model in which the Air Force installed improved air-to-ground capability with a new fire-control system, a lead-computing optical sight, ASG-63 inertial navigation system and the capability to handle "smart" bombs, guided to their targets by lasers or electro-optical means. Air Force men continued to make their best effort to use it to kill MiGs. This F-4D Phantom (66-7661) of the 435th TFS, part of the "Wolfpack" 8th TFW at Ubon, wears a red star on its splitter plate to signify a victory over a MiG-21. US Air Force

F-4C Phantom 63-7676 looks resplendent in Hawaii on July 29, 1984, with two MiG kills adorning its splitter plate. Unfortunately, although this Phantom fought through the conflict, the paired red stars were unearned. This particular Phantom never shot down a MiG. Robert F. Dorr

N010
MIKE CHOW A.C.
SKIP VINCENT W.S.O.
RESCUE
REMOVE BEFORE FLIGHT

PN
AF
50 704
OY
249

F-4D Phantom 65-704 of the 523rd TFS at Udorn, Thailand, on December 31, 1971. The Udorn airfield was especially vexing to fighter pilots because it had a massive dip in the center of the runway, necessitating some tricky handling to avoid a mishap on takeoff or landing. via Robert F. Dorr

When a MiG-21 became available to Air Force investigators in the late-1960s, they pooh-poohed the shoddy construction techniques, the bulging rivets which joined wing to fuselage and the outdated avionics. But the MiG-21 was evidence that while Soviet aircraft may appear crude, they do the job. The MiG-21bis was powered by a 16,500-lb. thrust Tumansky R-25 afterburning turbojet and armed with a twin-barrel 23-mm GSh-23 cannon, the kind of gun many Phantom pilots wished they had. It was one of the most successful and most numerous fighter aircraft in the world. Still, many of North Vietnam's best pilots preferred the older but more nimble MiG-17. Alain Pelletier

XN
AF
37 442
U.S. AIR FORCE

FOD

Previous page

Sitting on the ramp at Cam Ranh Bay, F-4C Phantom 63-7442 (XN) of the 359th TFS/12th TFW awaits a combat mission in February 1968. Richard Kamm

The F-4E Phantom came from the factory with the nose-installed 20 mm "Gatling gun" M39A1 cannon, designed to give the crew a better chance in a close-quarters gunfight with the MiG. Cannons accounted for forty-three air-to-air victories by American pilots. Had the F-4E been available before the October 31, 1968, termination of the Rolling Thunder campaign, the score might have been higher. F-4E Phantom 67-344 of the 3rd TFW at Clark Field, Philippines, taxies in. Peter Greve

RESCUE
0344

The "Gunfighters," the 366th TFW at Da Nang, built up an impressive combat record in air-to-ground and air-to-air combat. F-4E Phantom 68-306 (LC) of the 421st TFS/366th TFW stationed at Da Nang is seen during a visit to Ubon, Thailand, on August 24, 1971. At this juncture, pilots and crews were beginning to think they might get a second opportunity to conduct a major campaign over North Vietnam. via Robert F. Dorr

LC
AF
80
306
CAUTION

Following pages

Though restrictions against colorful markings on Phantoms were usually in force, Lt. Col. Edward Hillding made it known that he wanted shark's teeth on his squadron's aircraft, and after Hillding stood up to a four-star general on the issue, others followed suit. The F-4E Phantoms of the 34th TFS/388th TFW based at Korat were among the best-looking airplanes of the war but did not initially get a crack at the MiG because they arrived in the theater just after the bombing halt. via Hugh R. Muir

JJ
269

The manner in which a MiG kill was painted on an aircraft varied considerably from one unit to another. The practice got underway in the combat theater, was ignored when airplanes were repainted in later years, and underwent a resurgence in the 1970s and 1980s. F-4D Phantom 64-699 (HL) of the 388th TFW was a bona fide MiG killer and wore its red star without the usual yellow border when seen at Hill AFB, Utah, on July 27, 1977. Benjamin Knowles, Jr.

Survivors of the Vietnam conflict wore paint schemes never seen during the fighting. The "Coonass Militia" nickname of the Louisiana Air National Guard has aroused some criticism but seems to be firmly entrenched. F-4C Phantom 63-7704, another MiG killer, belongs to Louisiana and wears an experimental paint design used for maneuvers. The red star representing a MiG-17 shot down on May 14, 1967, stands out well against the gray. Phantom is shown here on May 6, 1983. Scott Wilson

Coonass Militia
AF
63
704
RESCUE

U.S. AIR FORC
USAF
91519
WISCON

Who are those guys?

The pilot of a Phantom or Thud might walk into a bar, throw his boot up on the rail and expect everybody to look at him as though he owned the place. He might, because heading north to fight the MiG was a romantic kind of endeavor out of *Dawn Patrol,* but every last man-jack in Southeast Asia knew that no MiGs would get shot down if it weren't for the hundreds of men and machines committed to difficult, risky and grueling support missions.

Reconnaissance, refueling and rescue were among the tasks which had to be performed if the fighters were going to get there, do their job and get back. Speaking of the Skyraider (or Sandy) which escorted rescue craft into North Vietnam and the RF-101C Voodoo reconnaissance planes which brought back target pictures, Colonel Robin Olds said, "No Sandy or Voodoo pilot was ever allowed to pay for a drink at the 0 Club at Ubon." The Phantom crews wouldn't permit it.

Some idea of the importance of the other guys can be gleaned from the composition of the force which participated in Olds' Operation Bolo, the January 2, 1967, effort which brought down seven MiG-21s in one day. To get the Phantoms in position to fight, six flights of F-105F Wild Weasels suppressed the enemy's SAM force. Several dozen KC-135 tankers worked in anchor orbit off the Vietnamese coast to provide life-giving fuel. Four flights of the little-used F-104C Starfighters prowled the coast to keep Ho Chi Minh from pulling any surprises.

As always, a rescue force stayed on alert, consisting of a C-130 Hercules command ship, A-1 Skyraiders in the escort or "Sandy role," and HH-3E Jolly Green Giant helicopters which flew the riskiest mission of all, darting through gunfire to pluck up any airman down inside North Vietnam. It didn't always work, but this kind of massive support force was supposed to give the MiG killers every chance to succeed and to live to fight again.

Previous page
The Boeing KC-135 Stratotanker was so vital to combat operations "up north" that tanker crews probably should have received some kind of official recognition each time a MiG was shot down. During the Korean War, air-to-air refueling had been attempted on a trial basis on a few combat missions. But Vietnam was the first conflict in which air refueling was routinely and consistently employed. More than once, when a battle-damaged fighter was low on fuel and leaking, a KC-135 "towed" it back to safety. Stratotankers were flown in combat by Strategic Air Command crews but many also served with the Air National Guard, including Wisconsin's KC-135E 59-1519, which has been re-engined with TF33 turbofans and is seen refueling Cessna 0A-37B on February 4, 1984. Douglas R. Tachauer

Before anyone could fly north to confront the MiG, photos of the enemy's lair were needed. The RF-101C Voodoo flew the bulk of the early reconnaissance missions over North Vietnam. Though it was not the fastest aircraft in the war, it flew the fastest missions. During one period at Udorn, the 20th TRS "Green Pythons" had fewer pilots than airplanes, but were required to mount two missions a day per aircraft. It was exhausting and dangerous work, but the Voodoo pilots brought home the pictures, providing much-needed intelligence on the enemy. Here, an RF-101C is preparing to start up at Udorn. John Bull Stirling

RESCUE

FORCE

To every fighter pilot who went north, it was a real comfort that Sandy was ready to help. The A-1 Skyraider wheezed, leaked oil and—with its R-3350 engine and paddle-bladed propeller at work—sounded like World War II revisited. But the Skyraider was also indispensable as an escort for rescue forces operating inside North Vietnam. Carrying out what became known as the Sandy mission, the A-1 used all manner of ordnance to keep the enemy's head down so that a rescue helicopter could get in to retrieve a man on the ground. Sometimes a Sandy got hit, too. Jim Rausch, center, is lucky to be safely back at Udorn on June 11, 1967, after his Skyraider was shot down and he was rescued inside North Vietnam. Robert L. Russell

Of the numerous aircraft which operated "up north," none was more important then the HH-3E Jolly Green Giant helicopter which existed solely for the purpose of rescuing downed airmen. Every pilot who flew in Ho Chi Minh's backyard was required to undergo survival training, called Snake School, in the Philippines in order to be able to handle himself when forced to evade the North Vietnamese army on the ground. This HH-3E is depicted at Snake School which derived its name from the men having to eat reptilian meat while in training. Later in the war, the HH-3E was supplanted by the larger HH-53C Super Jolly Green Giant. Arnie Franklin

The weather in North Vietnam was almost always terrible, with "soup" hanging in the valleys between the karst ridgelines. The HH-53C Super Jolly Green carried two pilots, a crew chief and two para-jumpers, or PJs, on its risky forays to rescue downed airmen. Between the bad weather, enemy gunfire and other threats, the HH-53C crew probably took more risks than anybody else in the conflict. On one occasion, an HH-53C was downed by a MiG. Another was shot down by a SAM missile. Dangerous work, but every fighter pilot admired the crews of these intrepid Sikorsky helicopters, and morale was greatly enhanced with the knowledge that they were part of the fight. US Air Force

USAF

It pays off—sometimes. RF-4C Phantom backseater Captain Ernest (Woody) Clark was on the ground in North Vietnam for nearly three days before rescue forces succeeded in pulling him out. The effort to rescue Clark involved A-1 Skyraiders, Phantoms, helicopters and tankers. Luckily, his April 1972 ordeal ended with a helicopter ride to Udorn (his frontseater was captured and taken prisoner), so Clark has much to be thankful about as he is greeted by squadron mates. Donald S. Pickard

From the beginning of the conflict to the end, some of the most dangerous missions were the unarmed photo-gathering flights carried out by the RF-8A and RF-8G reconnaissance variants of the Crusader. The Crusader was also the last dedicated recce aircraft to operate from carrier decks and remained in service until 1987. With its war behind, RF-8G Crusader 146882 of Reserve squadron VFP-306 awaits a flight at Andrews AFB, Maryland, on January 12, 1978. Robert F. Dorr

RESCUE
E
603
JET
DANGER
INTAKE

0 1
NOSE TIRES
150 PSI ASHORE

Linebacker

On March 30, 1972, North Vietnam launched its Easter invasion—a sudden and dramatic thrust to the south, using Reserve divisions which had not previously been committed to the conflict. The massive enemy offensive came as something of a surprise, at a time when the Nixon Administration had made progress toward reducing the US presence and winding down the war. Phantom pilots at Cam Ranh Bay were awakened by a sergeant who tore through the billets at 3:00 a.m., flashlight in hand, rousting everybody. "It's hit the fan!" the sergeant shouted. "They're coming down the pike with everything they've got!"

The invasion made it inevitable that US warplanes would have to return to North Vietnam to face an enemy force of missiles, MiGs and Triple-As which had been given three years to entrench itself. A few forays had been occurring "up north" already, one of the most dramatic being a February 21, 1972, mission in which F-4D Phantom pilot Major Bob

The "Tomcatters" of VF-31 were an East Coast-Atlantic Fleet squadron operating from USS Saratoga *(CVA-60) but they took their share of the burden in what many viewed as a West Coast-Pacific Fleet conflict. CDR Samuel C. Flynn, Jr., and Lt. William H. John were flying F-4J Phantom 157293 when they scored the squadron's only MiG kill, a MiG-21, on June 21, 1972. Their Phantom was duly inscribed with a silhouette of a MiG and an X to indicate that the MiG had been, so to speak, scratched out. In the postwar period, 157293 continued with VF-31 only long enough to be observed in a July 7, 1973, front view at NAS Kingsville, Texas, and was subsequently transferred to the "Red Rippers" of VF-11. To keep their history alive, the "Tomcatters" repainted another F-4J Phantom, 153769, in the paint scheme of the Flynn/John aircraft, replete with MiG kill. The later machine is seen at NAS Oceana, Virginia, on October 5, 1979.* Bob Thomas/Robert F. Dorr

101
JET
DANGER
INTAKE
RESCUE
101

101
AC
USS SARATOGA
VF-31
3769
153769
NAVY

Lodge and backseater 1st Lt. Roger Locher chased a MiG-21 up a valley at night and shot it down.

Now, a full-scale effort was due. On May 8, 1972, President Nixon announced the mining of Haiphong harbor and the return of American aircraft to the Hanoi-Haiphong region. The new campaign, reflecting the president's football interests, was named Linebacker.

Colonel Tomb and the men of the North Vietnamese air force were now well-trained and thoroughly ready. But the Americans, too, were well-prepared. Captain Frank Ault of the US Navy had conducted a review of air-to-air combat preparedness throughout the Fleet and his Ault Report had made no fewer than 241 recommendations to improve the Navy's readiness for air-to-air action. Most important of these was Ault's recommendation for air combat maneuver (ACM) training. This realistic dogfight training got under way at the Navy's Fighter Weapons School—Top Gun—and the Air Force soon developed a similar program.

On May 10, 1972, Air Force and Navy Phantom crews shot down no fewer than nine MiGs, suffering two losses. CDR Randall Cunningham and Lt. Willie P. Driscoll downed Colonel Tomb's MiG-17, racking up their fifth MiG kill to become the first aces of the war. The Air Force's three aces soon followed.

While all-out fighting went on simultaneously with efforts aimed at securing a peace agreement, Henry Kissinger announced that peace was at hand—but it wasn't, at least not quite. To persuade Hanoi to reach a settlement, the Nixon team launched the Eleven Day War of December 18-29, 1972, also known as Linebacker II, in which fully one-third of the entire SAC B-52 force was committed to around-the-clock bombing of key targets near Hanoi. The massive B-52 raids brought about the agreement that ended the conflict on January 27, 1973. They also added two MiG-21 kills by B-52 fire control operators (tailgunners) to the final roster of 195.

It has become almost cliche to point out that although the US lost the war in Vietnam, it won every contest on the field of battle. Cliche, but true. In the final days of the war, US airmen were shooting down up to six MiGs for every loss they suffered. There can be no doubt that American airpower inflicted a defeat upon the North Vietnamese Air Force. During the Linebacker and Linebacker II operations, the Phantoms and Stratofortresses won the battle. The MiG pilots knew it. Small wonder that pointed red stars began to appear on more and more Phantoms. In the final days, it was a one-sided rout.

Nobody had told the pilot of Chico, *F-4E Phantom 68-339 of the 388th Tactical Fighter Wing, that an F-4E was supposed to come armed with one 20-mm cannon.* Chico *went to war carrying no fewer than* three *external 20-mm cannon pods (one of which is seen mounted outboard in this view from the tanker) plus its internal gun and, in this instance, Rockeye cluster bombs. Lugging no fewer than four cannons through the blue,* Chico *would have been potent at strafing, but probably not maneuverable enough to bring its arsenal to bear on a MiG. This unusually armed fighter is seen on a strike in 1971, just before the Linebacker campaign was undertaken to renew missions against North Vietnam.* John Huggins

Several well-known MiG-killing crews flew F-4D Phantom 66-7463 of the 8th Tactical Fighter Wing, including Lt. Col. Joe Kittinger and Captain Richard S. (Steve) Ritchie who became the first Air Force ace of the war during the 1972 Linebacker campaign. Plane 463 accounted for six enemy aircraft, five MiG-21s and one MiG-19. No other aircraft flown by Americans was credited with more than three. At Korat on April 17, 1984, aircraft 463 had shed its original 0Y tailcode and acquired a WP, for "Wolfpack." David W. Menard

WP
463

FIELD ELEV
RETURN WITH HONOR

The six-kill F-4D Phantom 66-7463 wore its MiG kills in several styles and patterns. Many had hoped that this important aircraft would find its way to the Air Force Museum but in 1986 Air Force Secretary Edward Aldridge decided to display the Phantom out of doors at the academy at Colorado Springs. Plane 463 is seen here at Peterson AFB, Colorado, on November 24, 1986, arriving to be exhibited at the academy. R. B. Greby

Beyond any doubt, the pilot and weapons systems officer of an F-4 Phantom were expected to combine sharp reflexes and fast thinking with an almost mindboggling variety of skills. During the 1965-68 Rolling Thunder campaign, pilots tended to be older and many were veterans of World War II and Korea. In the 1972 fighting, pilots were younger, yet tended to be better-trained. This Hawaii Air National Guard crewman of an F-4C Phantom stands with an aircraft which served through the heaviest fighting and was retired from service only in 1987 when Hawaii received the F-15 Eagle. Robert F. Dorr

PN
AF
67
550

Previous page
On April 16, 1972, Major Edward D. (Don) Cherry and Captain Jeffrey S. Feinstein were flying F-4D Phantom 66-7550 of the 13th TFS/432nd TRW out of Udorn, callsign BASCO 03, when they used an AIM-7 Sparrow to shoot down a MiG-21. Feinstein went on to become the fifth ace of the Vietnam conflict with five confirmed aerial victories. The PN tailcode was on the aircraft at the time of the kill, although this view shows the Phantom a few months later at an airfield in Japan. via Robert F. Dorr

One of the best-cared-for double MiG killers of the war was F-4D Phantom 66-7554 which ended up with the Air Force Reserve's 89th TFS/906th TFG at Wright-Patterson AFB, Ohio, where it is depicted on April 1, 1984. On November 6, 1967, Captain Darrell D. Simmonds and 1st Lt. George H. McKinney, Jr., using callsign SAPPHIRE 01, used a centerline-mounted 20-mm gunpod to shoot down two MiG-17s. It is a tribute to the toughness and endurance of the Phantom that the aircraft was still in service, in seemingly pristine condition, two decades later. David W. Menard

DO
AF
66
554
AFRES

Cannon-armed F-4E Phantom 68-322 (JV) of the 469th TFS/388th TFW at Korat over Southeast Asia in March 1972, just as the war began to heat up again. Although pilots had wanted the internal 20-mm gun desperately, F-4E airplanes accounted for only twenty-three of the MiGs shot down in the conflict. via Michael A. France

After the Southeast Asia conflict, Phantoms began to appear in the lizard-green Europe One paint scheme. The purpose was to tone down the aircraft and make it less visible both to the human eye and to infrared devices. F-4E Phantom 68-338 of the 57th Fighter Weapons Wing at Nellis AFB, Nevada, defied this trend by wearing its MiG kill brightly on the port-side splitter plate. The red star indicates a MiG-21 downed with an AIM-9 Sidewinder on September 12, 1972, by Captain Calvin B. Tibbett and 1st Lt. William S. Hargrove. It was Tibbett's second kill. Marty J. Isham

WA
338
RESCUE

FA
00
AC
152946
NAVY
WT

Aircraft of all services flew and fought together when they had to, especially on high-altitude Sky Spot bombing missions which could easily be interrupted by MiGs. This combat view includes an Air Force F-4D Phantom from the 8th TFW and Marine Corps F-4J Phantoms of the "Red Devils" of VMFA-232. In the foreground is Grumman A-6A Intruder of VA-75. The bombs falling away appear to be 1,000-lb. Mark 84 high-explosive. US Navy

The "Fighting Falcons" of US Navy fighter squadron VF-96 operated from several carriers during the conflict but while aboard USS Constellation *(CVA-64) on May 10, 1972, the squadron produced the first aces of the war, F-4J pilot CDR Randall (Duke) Cunningham and his backseater Lt. Willie P. Driscoll. On that date, flying aircraft 155800, Cunningham and Driscoll bagged their third, fourth and fifth MiGs, the last-named being piloted by the enemy's much-publicized Colonel Tomb. F-4J Phantom 153819, seen near NAF Atsugi, Japan, on October 16, 1974, wears the same markings as did Cunningham's aircraft, which was finally shot down on the ace-making mission. Plane 155800 was hit by a SAM and went to the bottom of the Gulf of Tonkin while Cunningham and Driscoll ejected and were rescued.* Masumi Wada

The conflict behind, air ace CDR Randall Cunningham gets close to a MiG-17 on January 20, 1984. The museum aircraft is the same type as was piloted by Hanoi's Colonel Tomb when Cunningham blew him out of the sky to become an ace. Douglas E. Slowiak

The "Chargers" of VF-151 aboard USS Midway *(CVA-41) racked up six MiG kills during the Southeast Asia conflict, including the final kill of the war. This happened on January 12, 1973, when Lt. Victor Kovaleski and Lt. j.g. Geoffrey H. Ulrich, flying F-4J Phantom 155846, callsign DAKOTA, shot down a MiG-17. Kovaleski, incidentally, was shot down and rescued a couple of days later making him not only the war's final MiG killer but its final shootdown victim as well. The squadron's markings are well illustrated in this view of F-4J Phantom 155580, seen on June 13, 1978.* Masumi Wada

110

Following pages

The other Phantom squadron aboard USS Midway *was the "Fighting Vigilantes" of VF-151. This squadron was in many scrapes with North Vietnam's air force, but scored only one MiG kill. USS* Midway *later became the last US Navy carrier to operate Phantoms, having only recently converted to the F/A-18A Hornet. The markings shown in these views of F-4J Phantoms 155739 and 155579 remained essentially unchanged throughout the squadron's history with the Phantom.* Steve Daniels/Hideki Nagakubo

USS MIDWAY
NF
17
155739

16
NF
5579
USS
F-4J
155579
VF-151
NAVY

216
JET
DANGER
INTAKE

Following pages

F-4J Phantom 157267 was the aircraft in which Navy aces Randall Cunningham and Willie Driscoll shot down their first two MiGs. These were a MiG-21 downed on January 19, 1972, and a MiG-17 shot down on the first day of the Linebacker effort, May 8, 1972. After serving with the "Black Falcons" of VF-96, the aircraft was transferred to the "Aardvarks" of VF-114, another unit that fought extensively in the 1972 Linebacker campaigns. Still later, the Phantom was transferred again to Marine Corps squadron VMFA-122, another veteran. Joseph G. Handelman, DDS

S KITTYHAWK
CY 63
207

DC
7267
MARINES

MFA-122

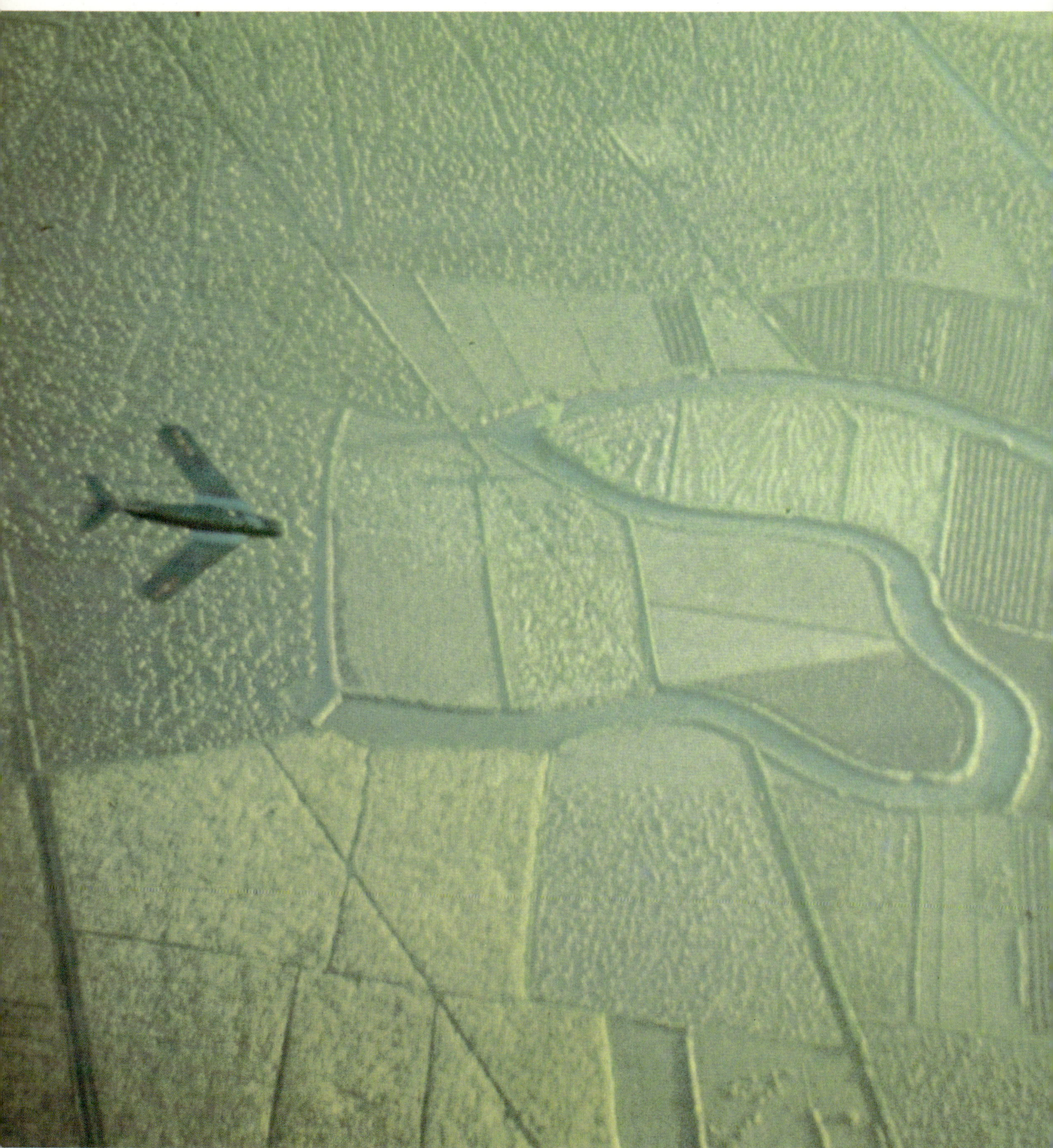

Gun-camera view of a MiG-17 under fire from a US Navy fighter on December 14, 1967. US Navy

RESCUE
CC
660

Veterans

The last Thud, the last Crusader have now made their final flights. The only Skyraiders left are on the airshow circuit, and the only Skyhawks are with a few squadrons yet to convert to newer craft. But it will be a long time before the last MiG killer of Vietnam goes off to that great boneyard in the sky. Phantoms and Stratofortresses will be with us for a long time to come. Numerous Phantoms have remained in service for more than twenty years after getting credit for a MiG.

F-4C Phantom 64-660, seen in no fewer than four views in this celebration, will soon be on permanent show at Niagara Falls with its trio of MiG kills happily displayed. The Air Force Museum in Dayton, Ohio, is taking good care of Colonel Robin Olds' F-4C Phantom 64-829, even if the Museum was unable to get hold of the six-kill F-4D Phantom, 66-7463. The Navy and Marine Corps have been noticeably less active in efforts to keep and preserve veterans of the conflict, but plans exist to display a MiG killer Phantom at the US Naval Aviation Museum, Pensacola, Florida.

Many of the individual aircraft which shot down MiGs were identified and suitably marked only in the 1970s and 1980s, and only then because of the efforts of a few historians like Tom Brewer, Bob Lawson and Bill Peake. The services themselves have not done nearly enough to identify, restore and preserve MiG killers, although the situation seems to be improving.

The guns are silent now. The last missile has been fired. But the MiG killers of the Southeast Asia conflict will remain very much a part of our world and our heritage. It can only be hoped that a future generation will have them to look at, that museums and history centers will keep alive this chapter of our most recent and longest war.

F-4C Phantom at Niagara Falls, New York. Don Linn

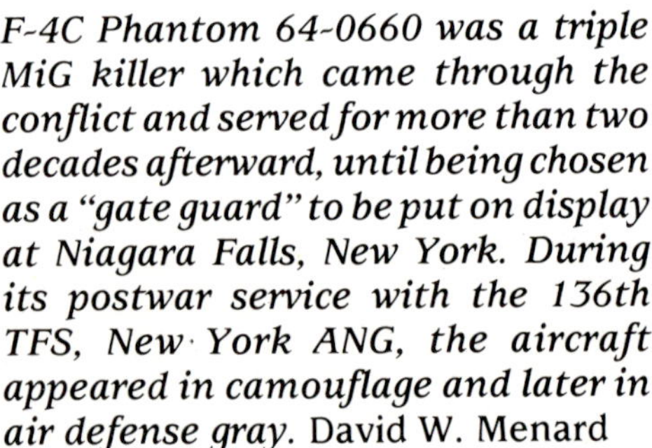
F-4C Phantom 64-0660 was a triple MiG killer which came through the conflict and served for more than two decades afterward, until being chosen as a "gate guard" to be put on display at Niagara Falls, New York. During its postwar service with the 136th TFS, New York ANG, the aircraft appeared in camouflage and later in air defense gray. David W. Menard

U.S. AIR FORCE
660

The Vietnam war ended on January 27, 1973, with the signing of a ceasefire but Americans remained in combat until the last mission was flown over Cambodia on August 15, 1973. The Phantom remained in Asia. The situation in Vietnam might have been resolved with the evacuation of Saigon on April 30, 1975, but the same fighters which had fought MiGs were now needed to cover US interests in the Philippines, Japan and Korea. Based at Clark Field, Philippines, is MiG-killing F-4E Phantom 68-0493 of the 3rd TFS/3rd TFW, seen on a visit to Misawa AB, Japan, on October 23, 1980. via Robert F. Dorr

PN
AF
80
493

RESCUE

OS
AF
69 297

Previous page
In Korea, the former MiG-fighters of the Vietnam conflict lie only a few minutes' flying time from more potential trouble. The 51st Tactical Fighter Wing at Korea's Osan AB is equipped with F-4E Phantoms which were employed in the conflict farther to the south, including aircraft 69-7297 seen on a visit to Yokota in 1983. Toshiki Kudo

While the war was going on, and afterward, the Phantom program continued at McDonnell Douglas' St. Louis facility. F-4E Phantom 69-7294 makes a test flight near St. Louis on December 1, 1970. The red-tipped device located in the bay normally employed for Sparrow missiles is a collision-avoidance warning instrument used on test flights but not operational missions. Production of the Phantom continued until 1978, with 5,201 examples of this famous fighter rolling off the production line. via Robert F. Dorr

USAF

Exactly 118 Phantoms were converted to carry out the Wild Weasel missions once performed by Thuds. These former F-4E aircraft were redesignated F-4G. Included was MiG killer 69-7235 of the 35th TFW, seen at George AFB, California, on November 9, 1980. via Robert F. Dorr

WW
AF
69 235
254

AF
093

The General Dynamics F-111A swing-wing fighter was briefly employed in Southeast Asia in 1968 during a deployment known as Combat Lancer which was far from successful. When it returned to the conflict in 1972, the much-maligned F-111A did a superb job and impressed airmen with the high accuracy of its precision, low-level bombing. Although it was called a fighter, the F-111A was never intended to do battle in the sky with the MiG, and no engagement occurred during the fighting. Arnie Franklin

No gallery of MiG killers is complete without the Boeing B-52D Stratofortress, the giant bomber which pulverized Hanoi and Haiphong during the Linebacker II operations of December 18-29, 1972. The B-52D Stratofortress at Maxwell AFB, Alabama, is remarkably well-preserved and is a fitting monument to the final days of the Vietnam conflict.

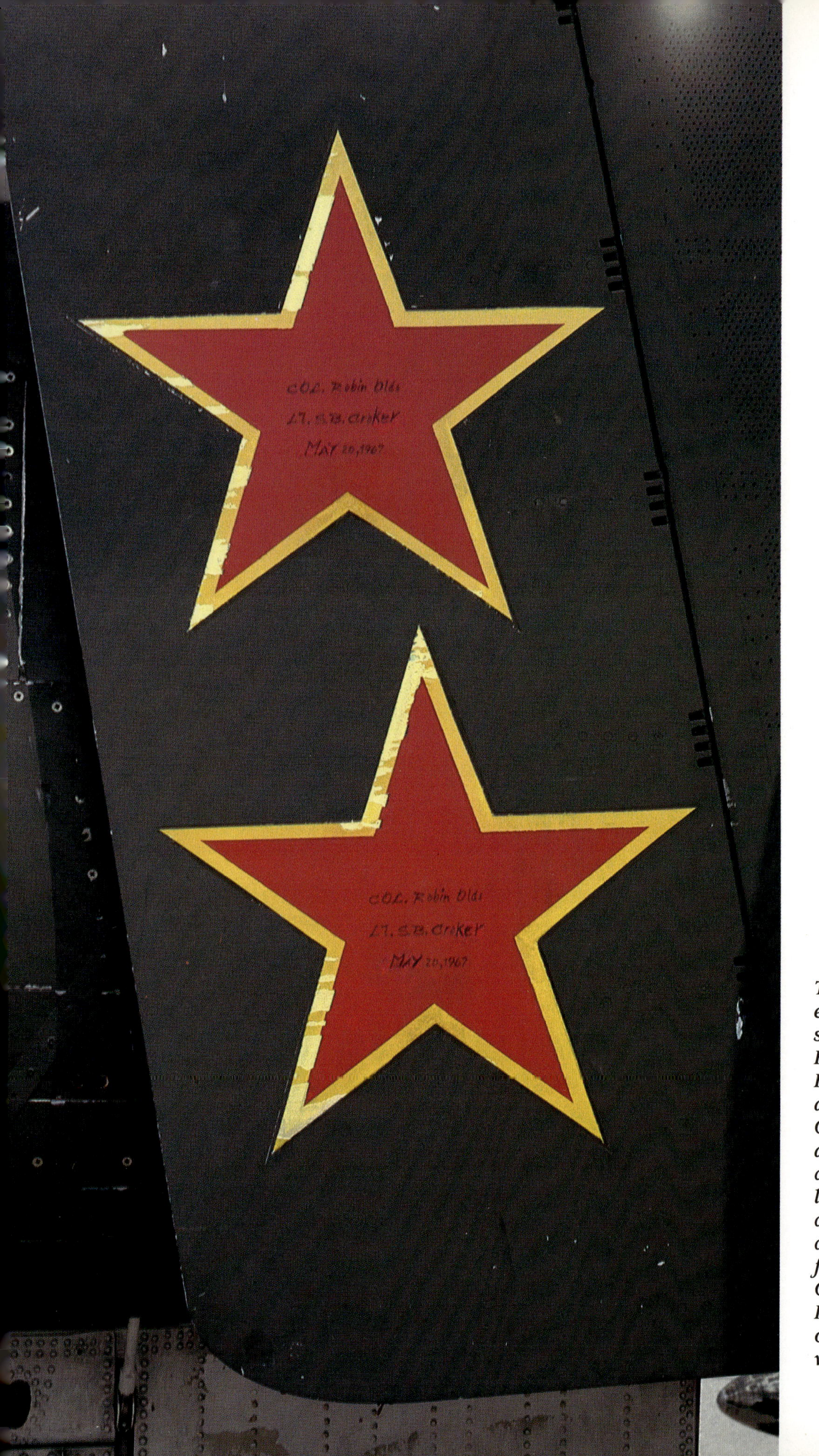

The story ends with yet another example of a MiG kill, a pair of red stars painted on Colonel Robin Olds' F-4C Phantom 64-829 at the Air Force Museum in Dayton, Ohio. Now a retired brigadier general, Robin Olds had a well-deserved reputation as a combat leader, picking the most dangerous missions for himself and leading his pilots against formidable defenses. But the four MiGs he shot down in Vietnam, two of them while flying this Phantom, were among Olds' most treasured achievements. In the end, every American who came out on top of the MiG felt the same way. David W. Menard